Questions AND Answers

DINOSAURS

Wendy Madgwick

KINGFISHER

NEW YORK

KINGFISHER
Larousse Kingfisher Chambers Inc.
95 Madison Avenue
New York, New York 10016

First published in 2000
10 9 8 7 6 5 4 3 2 1

1TR/0400/TIM/HBM/130MA

LIBRARY OF CONGRESS CATALOGING-IN-PUBLICATION DATA
has been applied for.

ISBN 0-7534-5309-6

Printed in China

Author: Wendy Madgwick
Designed, edited, and typeset by Tucker Slingsby Ltd.

Illustrations:
Marion Appleton, Richard Bonson, Jim Channel, Sandra Doyle, James Field,
Chris Forsey, Terry Gabby, Tim Hayward, Christian Hook, David Hurrel, Mark Iley,
Ian Jackson, Terence Lambert, Bernard Long, Shirley Mallinson, Robert Morton,
William Oliver, Roger Payne, Andrew Robinson, Eric Robson, Tim Slade, and
Ann Winterbotham
p.12 tl courtesy of the Department Library Services, American Museum of
Natural History, Neg. no. 410 764, Shackelford 1925

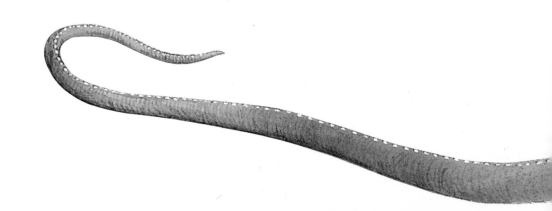

Contents

Digging up the Facts

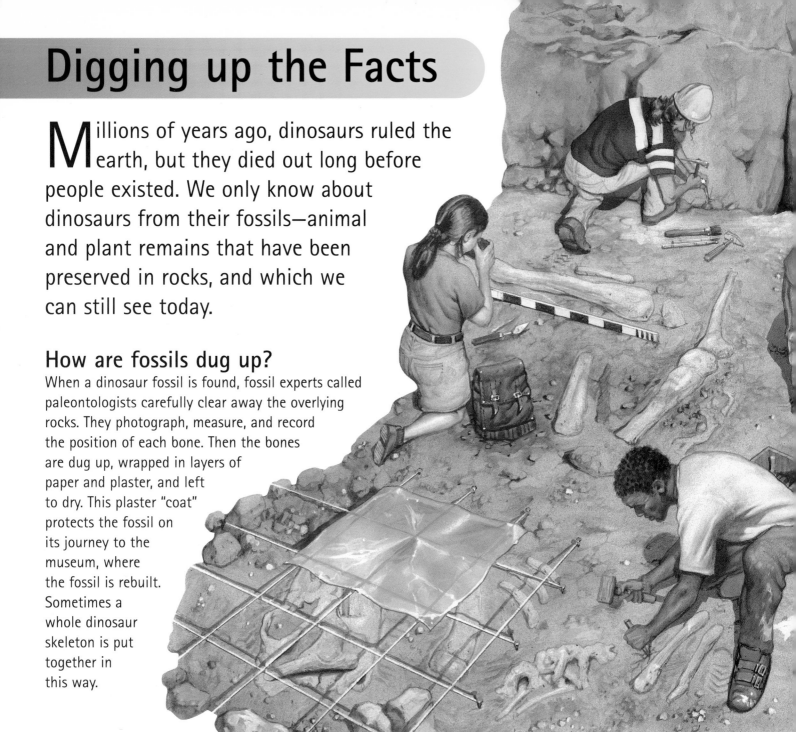

Millions of years ago, dinosaurs ruled the earth, but they died out long before people existed. We only know about dinosaurs from their fossils—animal and plant remains that have been preserved in rocks, and which we can still see today.

How are fossils dug up?

When a dinosaur fossil is found, fossil experts called paleontologists carefully clear away the overlying rocks. They photograph, measure, and record the position of each bone. Then the bones are dug up, wrapped in layers of paper and plaster, and left to dry. This plaster "coat" protects the fossil on its journey to the museum, where the fossil is rebuilt. Sometimes a whole dinosaur skeleton is put together in this way.

How is a fossil formed?

When an animal or plant dies, it usually rots away. However, if it is buried quickly by mud or sand, parts of it may survive. Over millions of years it will turn into a fossil.

1 A dinosaur dies, and its flesh is eaten or rots away.

2 Its skeleton is covered by layers of mud or sand.

3 Slowly, mud turns to rock, and bones become fossils.

4 As the rock wears away, the fossil is revealed.

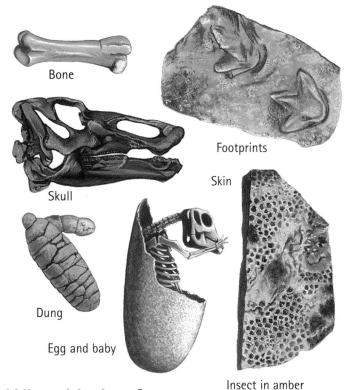

Bone

Skull

Dung

Egg and baby

Footprints

Skin

Insect in amber

Quick-fire Quiz

1. What are fossil experts called?
a) Fossiologists
b) Paleontologists
c) Rock collectors

2. Where are most fossils found?
a) Soil
b) Wood
c) Rock

3. Who invented the word "dinosaur"?
a) Mary Mantell
b) Edwin Cope
c) Richard Owen

4. What does *Megalosaurus* mean?
a) Fierce lizard
b) Big lizard
c) Toothed lizard

What kinds of fossils are there?

Fossilized bones and teeth are not the only dinosaur remains. Fossilized imprints of their scaly skin, footprints, and nests of eggs have all been found. Scientists can even tell what dinosaurs ate from their fossilized dung. Some fossils form in other ways. For example, an insect trapped in the sticky resin of a tree can be fossilized when the resin turns into hard amber.

George Cuvier

Mary Mantell

Gideon Mantell

Richard Owen

Edwin Cope

Othniel Marsh

William Buckland

One name or two?

Dinosaur names are in Latin and have two parts—the genus name and the species name. They are written in italics, and the genus name has a capital letter, as in *Tyrannosaurus rex*. Similar species are grouped in the same genus, which is the name usually used.

Who found the first dinosaur bones?

Dinosaur bones were first found hundreds of years ago, but people thought they were from giants or dragons. In 1822, Georges Cuvier suggested that they belonged to giant reptiles. In 1824, William Buckland named the first dinosaur, *Megalosaurus* ("big lizard"). Fossil hunters Mary and Gideon Mantell named a second dinosaur, *Iguanodon*, in 1825. Richard Owen first called them "dinosaurs" ("terrible lizards") in 1842. In America, over 130 kinds of dinosaurs were found by Edward Cope and Othniel Marsh.

Color and Camouflage

No one knows for sure what color dinosaurs were. A few pieces of fossilized dinosaur skin have been found, but the color faded millions of years ago. Perhaps they had similar colors to reptiles today.

What use are colors?

Deinonychus

Skin color can help animals hide, attract a mate, or send a warning to rivals. Like many animals today, some dinosaurs may have been camouflaged. This means their skin was patterned to blend in with their surroundings. For example, *Deinonychus* could have been sand-colored, like a modern lion, to blend in with the sandy ground or dry, yellow plants. Or perhaps it was striped, like a tiger, so that a pack could hide among the vegetation until it was ready to attack.

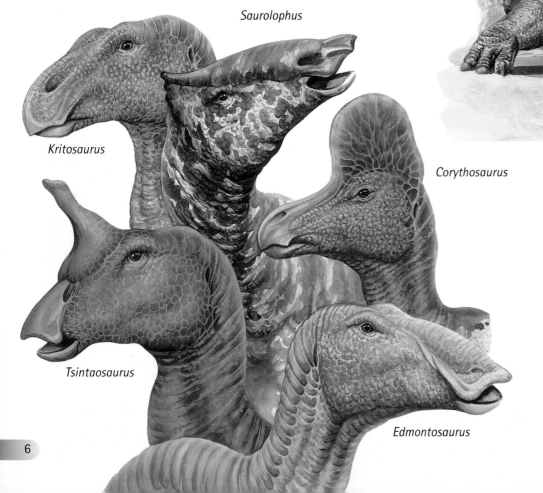

Saurolophus

Kritosaurus

Corythosaurus

Tsintaosaurus

Edmontosaurus

Could dinosaurs see in color?

No one knows for sure, but some probably could. We do know that some dinosaurs, called hadrosaurs, had crests, frills, and inflatable air sacs on their heads. The hadrosaurs' heads and crests were probably brightly colored so that they could be seen easily. Perhaps the dinosaurs also used their crests to send signals to each other. Several modern-day reptiles send signals in this way.

Were male and female dinosaurs different colors?

Mallard ducks

It is highly possible that they were. The male and female adults of many animals today, including some birds and lizards, are colored differently. The male may use his bright colors to attract a female or to warn other males to stay away. Females may have dull, drab colors so they are harder to spot when sitting on eggs or looking after babies. When artists first started drawing dinosaurs, they tended to make them all brown or green, but now dinosaurs are often shown with very colorful markings.

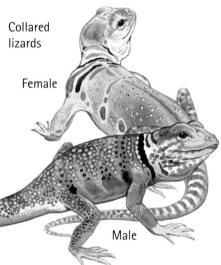

Collared lizards

Female

Male

Parasaurolophus

Male

Female

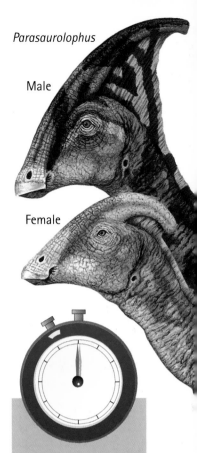

Quick-fire Quiz

1. Which of these had a large crest?
   a) *Deinonychus*
   b) *Corythosaurus*
   c) *Kritosaurus*

2. Why was dinosaur skin bumpy?
   a) For protection
   b) For warmth
   c) For camouflage

3. Why might dinosaurs have had stripes?
   a) To show off
   b) To confuse predators
   c) To attract mates

4. What is camouflage?
   a) Blending in with the surroundings
   b) Changing color
   c) Having bright warning colors

Why would dinosaurs be striped?

A zebra's stripes break up its outline, making it hard for a predator to pick one animal out from the herd. Dinosaurs that lived in herds may have had stripes for the same reason.

Smooth or scaly?

Fossils and fossilized skin show that many dinosaurs were covered with lumps and bumps for protection. Several colorful reptiles today have similar skin, so some experts think dinosaurs were also brightly colored.

7

Dinosaur Giants

Dinosaurs are the biggest land animals that have ever lived on earth. The largest dinosaurs were the plant-eating sauropods. There were several kinds, but they all had enormous bodies, long necks, and small heads. Some were as tall as a four-story building.

Which was the heaviest dinosaur?

Only a few bones of *Supersaurus* and *Ultrasaurus* have been found, but they both outweigh *Brachiosaurus*. *Ultrasaurus* holds the record at almost 100 feet long, 40 feet high, and up to 130 tons in weight. That is as heavy as 20 large elephants.

Which is the largest dinosaur skeleton?

The biggest almost-complete skeleton found so far is that of *Brachiosaurus*. This dinosaur was so tall it could raise its head 43 feet above the ground. One *Brachiosaurus* would have weighed as much as ten large elephants.

Brachiosaurus

Diplodocus

Apatosaurus

The huge sauropods were many times bigger than today's largest land animal, the elephant.

Which dinosaurs had the heaviest bones?

Sauropod dinosaurs had the biggest and heaviest bones. A thigh bone weighing 992 pounds has been found. Early fossil-hunters struggled to get their finds home. Today, helicopters are often used.

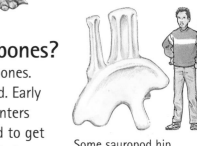

Some sauropod hip bones are bigger than an adult man.

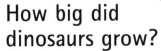

Were dinosaurs smart?

Dinosaurs may have been big, but they were not all very smart. Most of them, like this *Stegosaurus,* had a small brain. For its size, *Brachiosaurus* had the smallest brain of almost any known dinosaur. Its brain weighed only $1/100,000$ of its body weight. You are much brainier: a human brain weighs $1/40$ of an adult's body weight. But fossils show us that some dinosaurs had much bigger brains and were probably more intelligent.

How big did dinosaurs grow?

It is hard to figure out the size of the biggest dinosaurs because only a few bones have been found. Experts think that *Ultrasaurus* was the heaviest and that *Seismosaurus* was the longest (128–170 feet). That's longer than a blue whale—the biggest animal alive today.

Blue whale

Which was the biggest carnivore?

Tyrannosaurus rex was one of the biggest meat-eating dinosaurs. It grew up to 45 feet long and over 16 feet high. Its head alone was over 3 feet long. It could have opened its mouth wide enough to swallow you whole!

Which dinosaur had the biggest feet?

The front feet of sauropods such as *Brachiosaurus* were huge—up to 3 feet long. Some fossilized sauropod footprints are big enough to sit in. A sauropod's feet had to be big to support the dinosaur's great weight. Paleontologists can figure out an animal's size, weight, and speed from its footprints.

No dinosaur could ever really have lived like this.

Did dinosaurs live under water?

People once thought that *Brachiosaurus* was too big to live on land. They thought it supported its weight by living in water and breathing through the nostrils on the top of its head. We now know this is not true. The pressure of the water would have crushed its ribs and kept *Brachiosaurus* from breathing.

Quick-fire Quiz

1. How long was *Tyrannosaurus rex's* head?
a) 3 feet
b) 13 feet
c) 30 feet

2. Which dinosaurs lived under water?
a) None of them
b) *Stegosaurus*
c) *Brachiosaurus*

3. Which is the most complete sauropod skeleton?
a) *Brachiosaurus*
b) *Tyrannosaurus*
c) *Ultrasaurus*

4. What is the biggest animal alive today?
a) Elephant
b) *Seismosaurus*
c) Blue whale

Small Dinosaurs

Not all dinosaurs were huge. Some were as small as modern-day lizards. Fewer fossils of small dinosaurs have been found because they were often eaten by other dinosaurs and their fragile bones were easily broken.

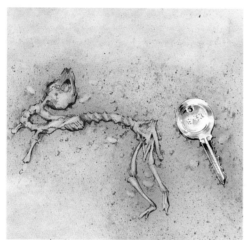

What is the smallest dinosaur skeleton?

A *Mussaurus* ("mouse-lizard") skeleton found in Argentina in South America was tiny enough to fit into the palm of your hand. The skeleton was a baby dinosaur with a big head, eyes, and feet. Small eggs, about an inch long, were found nearby. An adult *Mussaurus* would have been about 10 feet long.

What did small dinosaurs eat?

1 Some small dinosaurs ate plants, while others fed on insects, worms, or small reptiles. Tiny *Lesothosaurus* lived in herds and fed on plants. It relied on speed to outrun predators.

Which were the smallest dinosaurs?

One of the earliest and smallest meat-eating dinosaurs was *Saltopus*. At just 24 inches long, its body was the same size as that of a large chicken. *Saltopus* was a speedy hunter and could catch fast-moving lizards and flying insects. In 1984, a small plant-eating dinosaur, *Leaellynasaura*, was found in Australia. It was about the same size as *Saltopus*. However, some scientists think that the fossils were not fully grown and that adult *Leaellynasaura* may have been up to 7 feet long.

Leaellynasaura

Saltopus

2 *Compsognathus* was the size of a large pet cat. It moved quickly, using its speed to catch fast-moving prey like insects and lizards. One *Compsognathus* skeleton has been found with the remains of its last meal, a lizard, inside it.

3 *Hypsilophodon* was a speedy little dinosaur that grew to about 7 feet long. It lived in forests and used its horny beak to nip off juicy shoots from plants.

4 Wolf-sized *Oviraptor* may have darted along at up to 30 miles per hour. It hunted lizards and small mammals and raided other dinosaurs' nests to snatch the eggs.

How big were dinosaur babies?

Newly hatched dinosaur babies were very small. You could have held this baby *Protoceratop*s in your hand. One baby *Troodon* fossil has been found that is only 3 inches long—the size of a large hen's egg.

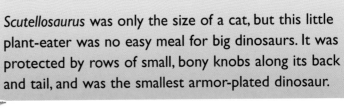

Did small dinosaurs defend themselves?

Scutellosaurus was only the size of a cat, but this little plant-eater was no easy meal for big dinosaurs. It was protected by rows of small, bony knobs along its back and tail, and was the smallest armor-plated dinosaur.

Dinosaur Babies

For centuries, scientists puzzled over how dinosaur babies were born. Then, in 1923, an expedition to the Gobi Desert in Mongolia found a nest of fossilized dinosaur eggs, laid over 100 million years earlier. This proved that dinosaurs hatched from eggs.

Who found the first eggs?

Roy Chapman Andrews discovered the first dinosaur eggs in 1923 in the Gobi Desert. He worked for the American Museum of Natural History and led many exciting dinosaur-hunting expeditions. His team also discovered the remains of *Baluchitherium*, the largest land mammal that ever lived.

How big were dinosaur eggs?

Dinosaur eggs were laid in groups of ten to 40. The size of the egg varied according to the size of the adult, but they were small for such large animals. For example, a 100-foot-long female probably laid eggs about 25 inches long. A really huge egg would need such a thick shell that a baby could not break out of it.

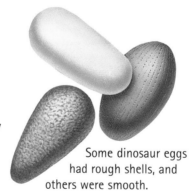

Some dinosaur eggs had rough shells, and others were smooth.

Did dinosaurs build nests?

Did dinosaurs look after their babies?

Experts think that some kinds of baby dinosaurs, such as young *Maiasaura*, were not very well developed. The adults probably fed their newly hatched young on soft plant shoots until they were able to fend for themselves. The babies of other dinosaurs, such as *Orodromeus*, were well developed and could probably run soon after they hatched. So perhaps, like many reptiles today, these dinosaurs laid lots of eggs and left their hatchlings to look after themselves.

1 Some dinosaurs, such as the *Maiasaura* shown here, built nests. *Maiasaura* lived in herds. Every year the females gathered at the same nesting site. We know this because a huge nesting area has been found in Montana.

2 Female *Maiasaura* made low mounds of mud about 6 feet across. Each female dug out a nest and lined it with twigs and leaves.

Did dinosaurs sit on their eggs?

In 1993, an expedition in the Gobi Desert discovered the fossilized remains of an *Oviraptor* sitting on a nest of eggs. The find proved that some dinosaurs sat on their eggs to hatch them, in the same way that birds do today.

Quick-fire Quiz

1. Where were the first eggs found?
a) Sahara Desert
b) Gobi Desert
c) Kalahari Desert

2. Which dinosaur stole eggs?
a) *Troodon*
b) *Triceratops*
c) *Maiasaura*

3. Who found the first eggs?
a) Indiana Jones
b) Richard Owen
c) Roy Chapman Andrews

4. What were *Maiasaura* nests made of?
a) Stones
b) Mud
c) Paper

Did dinosaurs protect their young?

Armored dinosaurs like *Triceratops* may have defended their young by charging a would-be predator. Scientists think a herd of adult plant-eaters on the move defended their young by keeping them in the middle of the group.

3 Each female laid about 20 to 25 eggs in the nest. She covered them with plants to keep them warm.

4 The *Maiasaura* mother guarded her eggs carefully. Egg-thieves, such as *Troodon*, were always ready to snatch an easy meal.

5 The *Maiasaura* hatchlings broke out of their shells using a special, sharp tooth on their snouts.

Communication

Animals cannot talk to each other, so they communicate in other ways. They use sounds, smells, touch, and visual signals to tell each other what is going on. Dinosaurs may have used similar methods to "talk" to one another.

What sounds did dinosaurs make?

Dinosaurs had complex ears and could probably hear well, so they may have used many different sounds to send signals to each other. Like reptiles today, most dinosaurs could probably hiss or grunt, and large ones may have roared. A few, like the hadrosaurs, probably made distinctive calls to each other through their horns, crests, and inflatable nose flaps. Scientists believe this is possible because when they blew through models of different hadrosaur skulls, they found that each skull made a different sound.

Tsintaosaurus

Edmontosaurus

Corythosaurus

Male peacock displaying

Lambeosaurus

Why was making a noise useful?

Dinosaurs may have used sound to warn of danger or to keep in touch with other members of a large herd. *Parasaurolophus* may have hooted a warning if danger threatened. The duck-billed dinosaur *Edmontosaurus* may have blown up a bag of skin over its nose and bellowed loudly at rival males. Young dinosaurs may have squeaked to get an adult's attention.

Did dinosaurs display like birds?

Experts think that some male dinosaurs displayed to the females during the mating season. Just as peacocks display their colored feathers, male dinosaurs may have displayed bright head crests, spines, or neck ruffs to attract females and ward off rival males.

Did dinosaurs use their noses?

Fossils of dinosaurs' brains suggest that many dinosaurs had a good sense of smell and that most had well-developed nostrils. A strong sense of smell would have helped dinosaurs sniff out food. If, as some scientists think, dinosaurs gave off scent signals, they may also have used their sense of smell to find a mate. *Brachiosaurus* had huge nostrils on the top of its head. No one knows why, but perhaps they allowed the dinosaur to eat water plants and breathe at the same time.

Brachiosaurus

Parasaurolophus herd

Quick-fire Quiz

1. Which dinosaur group had head crests?
   a) Hadrosaurs
   b) Theropods
   c) Lizards

2. Which dinosaur had an inflatable nose flap?
   a) *Edmontosaurus*
   b) *Brachiosaurus*
   c) *Lambeosaurus*

3. Which dinosaur had a hollow crest?
   a) *Tyrannosaurus*
   b) *Brachiosaurus*
   c) *Parasaurolophus*

4. Where were *Brachiosaurus's* nostrils?
   a) On the end of its nose
   b) On top of its head
   c) It didn't have any

How did noisy noses work?

Hadrosaurs such as *Parasaurolophus* and *Lambeosaurus* had hollow crests. Air passages extended from the nose, through the crest, and down into the throat. The dinosaurs could hoot and honk as they breathed in and out. Different types of crests produced different notes.

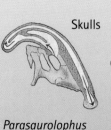 

Skulls

Parasaurolophus   *Lambeosaurus*

Could dinosaurs taste their food?

Many dinosaurs had tongues, and they could probably taste and smell their food, like most animals today. Reptiles such as snakes use their forked tongue to "taste" the air for traces of prey. But there is no evidence to suggest that any dinosaurs had tongues that could do this.

Plant-eaters

Most dinosaurs were herbivores. This means they ate only plants. Plant-eating dinosaurs came in all shapes and sizes, from small, two-legged dinosaurs to huge sauropods. Plants are hard to digest, so to get enough energy from their food, many spent most of the day eating.

Psittacosaurus

Lizard or bird hips?

Experts divide dinosaurs into two groups by the shape of their hips. Sauropod plant-eaters

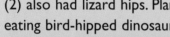

1 (1) had lizard hips. Their big stomachs unbalanced them, so they had to walk on four legs. Two-legged theropod meat-eaters
2 (2) also had lizard hips. Plant-eating bird-hipped dinosaurs
3 (3) evolved later. Many walked on two legs with their big stomach slung between their back legs. Armored bird-hipped plant-eaters were so heavy that they walked on four legs.

Did dinosaurs eat leaves?

Leaves were the main diet of many plant-eaters. *Psittacosaurus* probably snipped leaves off with its birdlike beak, then sliced them into smaller bits with its scissorlike teeth. Like the giraffe, *Brachiosaurus* used its long neck to graze on leafy treetops.

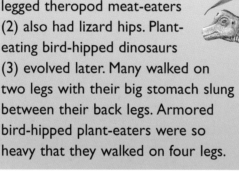

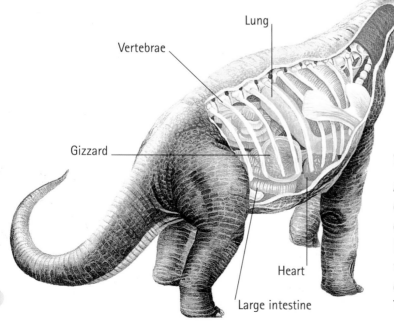

Lung

Vertebrae

Gizzard

Heart

Large intestine

Why were sauropods so big?

A sauropod's huge body was filled almost entirely with its organs. Sauropods like *Brachiosaurus* ate up to 450 pounds of plants a day, so they needed a big stomach and long intestines to digest this tough food. Experts had to guess what a dinosaur's insides looked like until 1998, when two dinosaurs from China were found with their organs intact. These should tell us more about what dinosaurs ate.

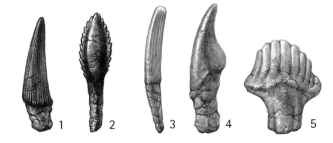

Lufengosaurus

1 2 3 4 5

Did plant-eaters have teeth?

Most plant-eating dinosaurs had teeth, and experts can tell what food a dinosaur ate by looking at them. *Lufengosaurus*, an early sauropod, had many small, peglike teeth with jagged edges. These were great for nipping off soft leaves, but no use for chewing, so *Lufengosaurus* swallowed its food whole.

Why were teeth different shapes?

The size and shape of a dinosaur's teeth depended on what it ate. The ornithopod *Heterodontosaurus* had sharp, narrow front teeth (1) for cutting and slicing. *Plateosaurus* (2) and sauropods like *Diplodocus* (3) and *Apatosaurus* (4) had peglike teeth to shred and crush food. *Stegosaurus* (5) had leaf-shaped teeth for slicing and munching soft plants.

Why did dinosaurs swallow stones?

Small stones have been found in the ribcages of many dinosaurs. Few dinosaurs could move their jaws from side to side, so they could not chew their food. They swallowed it whole and probably swallowed small stones, called gastroliths, to help them grind food as it churned in their stomachs. Chickens swallow grit to do the same thing.

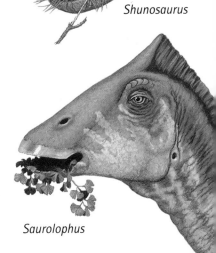

Shunosaurus

Quick-fire Quiz

1. What are gastroliths?
a) Grinding teeth
b) Stomach stones
c) Plants

2. Which dinosaur had leaf-shaped teeth?
a) *Diplodocus*
b) *Apatosaurus*
c) *Stegosaurus*

3. Which dinosaur had a birdlike beak?
a) *Shunosaurus*
b) *Brachiosaurus*
c) *Psittacosaurus*

4. What did *Triceratops* eat?
a) Fruit and nuts
b) Ferns and horsetails
c) Grass

Did dinosaurs eat grass?

Grasses did not develop on earth until 25 million years after the dinosaurs died out. Instead, herbivorous dinosaurs ate other plants that were around at the time. Long-necked sauropods such as *Shunosaurus* used their simple, peglike teeth to munch on leaves, pine needles, and juicy shoots. A hadrosaur such as *Saurolophus* ate leaves from flowering plants and crunchy pinecones. It chopped off the leaves with its horny beak, then chewed them with its flat back teeth. Horned dinosaurs like *Triceratops* sliced up tough ferns and horsetails with their sharp beaks and teeth.

Leaves, pine needles, and shoots

Pinecones and shrub leaves

Ferns and horsetails

Saurolophus

Triceratops

17

Meat-eaters

All meat-eating, or carnivorous, dinosaurs were theropods. (Theropod means "beast foot.") They walked on two legs, and their three toes were armed with sharp claws. Some were fierce hunters, chasing and killing their prey. Others were scavengers, feeding on dead animals.

Did dinosaurs have sharp teeth?

The sharp, backward-pointing teeth of *Megalosaurus* are typical of many large meat-eating dinosaurs. They were good for gripping and ripping their prey. Other carnivorous dinosaurs had small, sharp teeth or crushing beaks.

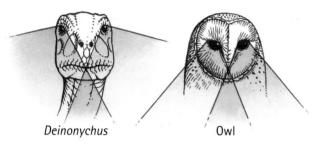

Deinonychus   Owl

Did meat-eaters have sharp eyesight?

Many hunters, such as *Deinonychus*, had good eyesight. It may have had forward-facing eyes and good binocular (overlapping) vision, like modern owls. This would have given it a single view of its prey and helped it judge distances.

Did all meat-eaters look alike?

Meat-eating dinosaurs came in all shapes and sizes. They ranged from chicken-sized *Saltopus* (24 inches) to huge *Tyrannosaurus* (40 feet long). Big theropods like *Tyrannosaurus*, *Allosaurus*, and *Dilophosaurus* hunted large plant-eaters, while speedy *Troodon* killed small reptiles and mammals. *Struthiomimus*, *Avimimus*, and *Oviraptor* used their strong beaks to catch and crush insects and eggs.

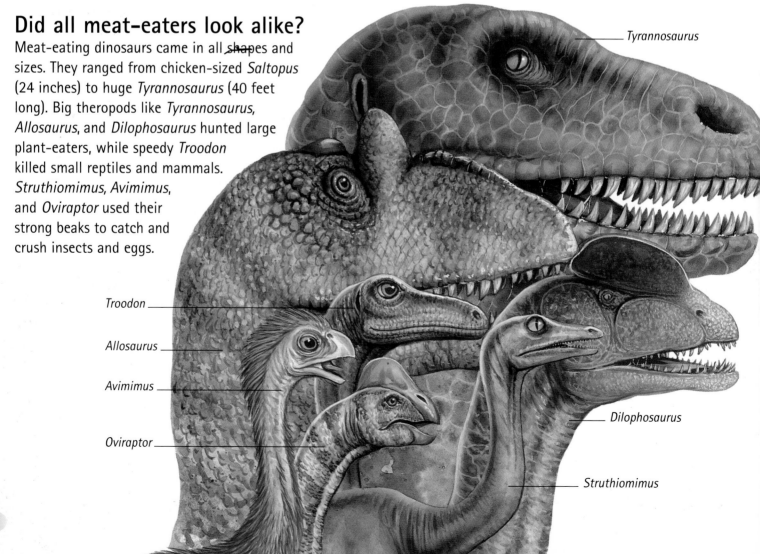

Tyrannosaurus

Troodon

Allosaurus

Avimimus

Oviraptor

Dilophosaurus

Struthiomimus

Did dinosaurs eat fish?

Experts believe that dinosaurs such as *Baryonyx* snapped up fish with their long, crocodile-like jaws. *Baryonyx* may also have speared fish with the huge, hooklike claws on its front feet, just as brown bears do today.

Which dinosaurs used claws to kill?

Deinonychus ("terrible claw") and its relatives specialized in using their claws to kill animals much larger than themselves. *Deinonychus* leapt at its victims, slashing them with the deadly, 5-inch claw on the second toe of its back foot.

Did dinosaurs hunt in packs?

Like today's wolves, some small meat-eating dinosaurs, such as *Deinonychus,* hunted in packs. This would have allowed them to hunt larger prey, such as a young *Diplodocus,* separating it from the rest of its herd.

Quick-fire Quiz

1. Which dinosaur was a cannibal?
a) *Diplodocus*
b) *Dilophosaurus*
c) *Coelophysis*

2. Which dinosaur ate fish?
a) *Oviraptor*
b) *Allosaurus*
c) *Baryonyx*

3. Which dinosaur name means "terrible claw"?
a) *Troodon*
b) *Deinonychus*
c) *Tyrannosaurus*

4. What did scavengers eat?
a) Dead animals
b) Bark
c) Leaves

Wolf pack

Were any dinosaurs cannibals?

Fossil remains of *Coelophysis* found in New Mexico had skeletons of young ones inside them. The bones were too big to belong to unborn *Coelophysis.* Experts believe that adult *Coelophysis* would eat their own young if food was short. Other dinosaurs may have been cannibals, too.

Did dinosaurs eat eggs?

Small, speedy meat-eaters such as *Troodon* snatched unguarded eggs from other dinosaurs' nests. Eggs were a good source of food— a complete meal in a shell! *Troodon* could sprint at about 30 miles per hour, so few lumbering plant-eaters could catch it.

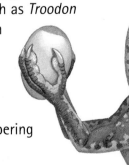

The Fiercest Dinosaur

Tyrannosaurus rex ("king tyrant lizard") lived about 70 million years ago. At over 40 feet long and three times as tall as a man, it was one of the largest and deadliest creatures that has ever lived on land.

Has a whole *Tyrannosaurus* skeleton ever been found?

Complete fossil skeletons are very rare, but in 1990, two almost complete *Tyrannosaurus* skeletons were found in the United States. Experts studying *Tyrannosaurus* skeletons believe that, unlike modern meat-eaters such as lions and tigers, the female *Tyrannosaurus* was probably bigger than the male.

Did *Tyrannosaurus* grasp prey with its front legs?

Tyrannosaurus's arms and hands were too small to grasp its prey. They couldn't even reach its mouth. Its head and teeth were so strong and deadly that it did not need its arms to catch its prey.

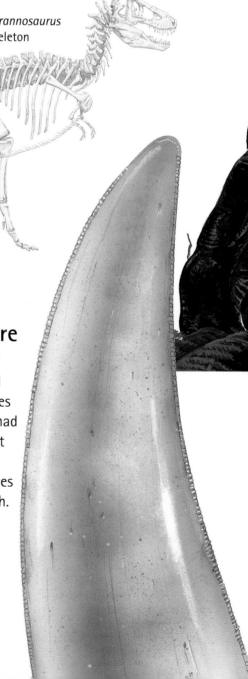

Tyrannosaurus skeleton

Dilophosaurus

Allosaurus

Albertosaurus

How big were *T. rex* teeth?

Tyrannosaurus had teeth up to 7 inches long. These teeth had a razor-sharp point to stab prey, and rough, sawlike edges to rip through flesh. An adult had between 50 and 100 teeth. If one fell out, it simply grew another!

Were there other big meat-eaters?

The three meat-eaters above were related to *Tyrannosaurus*, but were not as big. Two huge, 8.5-foot-long fossil arms with clawed hands were found in Mongolia and named *Deinocheirus* ("terrible hand"). They may be from a species of *Deinonychus* that was even bigger than *Tyrannosaurus*.

Quick-fire Quiz

1. How long ago did *Tyrannosaurus* live?
a) 7 million years
b) 70 million years
c) 170 million years

2. How long were its teeth?
a) Up to 2 inches
b) Up to 5 inches
c) Up to 7 inches

3. Which dinosaur was related to *Tyrannosaurus*?
a) *Triceratops*
b) *Albertosaurus*
c) *Deinocheirus*

4. What does "*Tyrannosaurus rex*" mean?
a) Big, bad lizard
b) King tyrant lizard
c) Emperor reptile

Was *Tyrannosaurus* fast or slow?

Experts used to think that *Tyrannosaurus* stood upright and lumbered along, dragging its tail on the ground. By studying the more complete skeletons, they now think it leaned forward, with its tail sticking out as a balance, and that it could run fast. Judging from its skull and the size of its brain, experts think it also had good eyesight and hearing and an excellent sense of smell.

Wrong   Right

Was the fiercest dinosaur a scavenger?

Some experts think *Tyrannosaurus* was a scavenger that ate dead animals and stole prey from other predators. Others think it could run as fast as a racehorse (30 miles per hour) and was a fierce hunter. The latest finds show it probably did both.

Attack and Defense

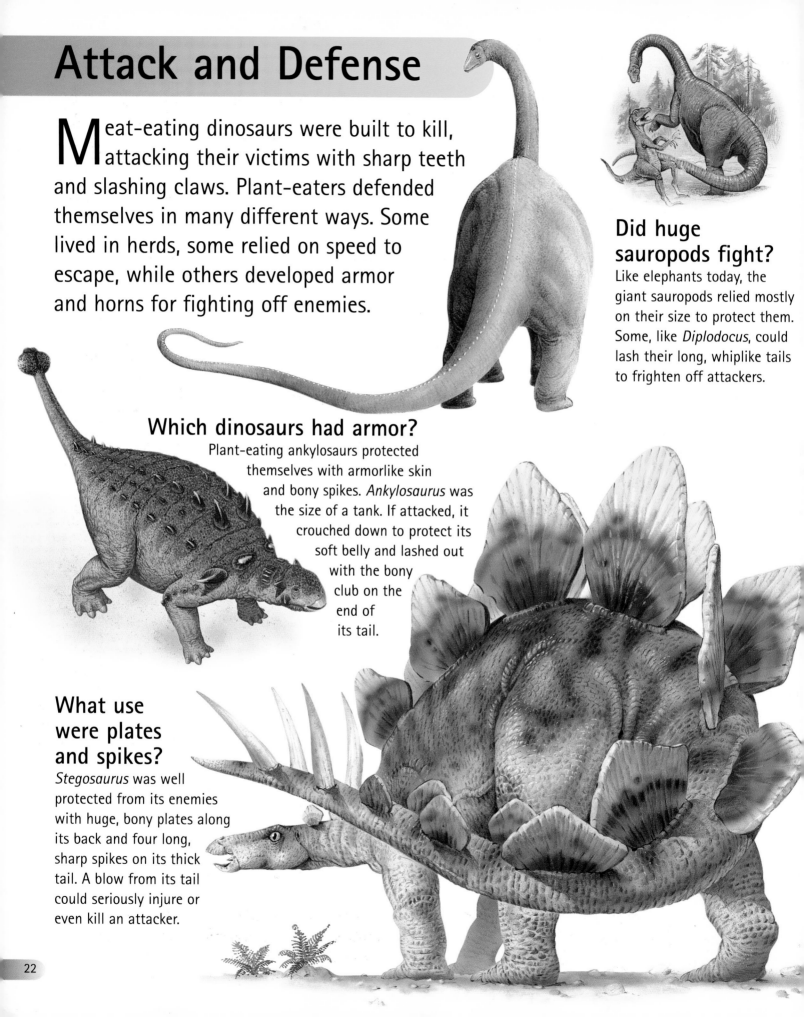

Meat-eating dinosaurs were built to kill, attacking their victims with sharp teeth and slashing claws. Plant-eaters defended themselves in many different ways. Some lived in herds, some relied on speed to escape, while others developed armor and horns for fighting off enemies.

Did huge sauropods fight?

Like elephants today, the giant sauropods relied mostly on their size to protect them. Some, like *Diplodocus*, could lash their long, whiplike tails to frighten off attackers.

Which dinosaurs had armor?

Plant-eating ankylosaurs protected themselves with armorlike skin and bony spikes. *Ankylosaurus* was the size of a tank. If attacked, it crouched down to protect its soft belly and lashed out with the bony club on the end of its tail.

What use were plates and spikes?

Stegosaurus was well protected from its enemies with huge, bony plates along its back and four long, sharp spikes on its thick tail. A blow from its tail could seriously injure or even kill an attacker.

Armor or radiators?

The plates along the back of *Stegosaurus* were covered with skin and had a lot of blood vessels in them. Some experts think they may have helped the dinosaur warm its body when it basked in the sun, and cool down by losing heat quickly in the shade. Other scientists think the plates were armor to protect it from carnosaurs (meat-eating dinosaurs) such as *Tyrannosaurus*.

Did plant-eaters have claws?

Most did not, but the plant-eating *Iguanodon* had two sharp thumb spikes. Perhaps it used them to stab attackers. Or maybe the males used them to fight each other.

Which dinosaurs had horns?

Plant-eating dinosaurs called ceratopsians developed horns and bony frills to protect themselves. They may have charged at enemies as a rhinoceros does, or maybe rival males fought by locking horns.

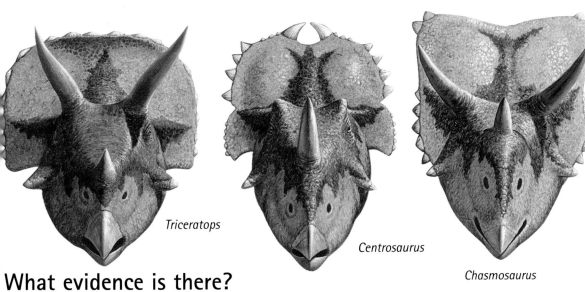

Triceratops

Centrosaurus

Chasmosaurus

Quick-fire Quiz

1. Which dinosaur had plates and spikes?
a) *Stegosaurus*
b) *Diplodocus*
c) *Tyrannosaurus*

2. Which dinosaur had a tail club?
a) *Velociraptor*
b) *Ankylosaurus*
c) *Diplodocus*

3. How did *Iguanodon* protect itself?
a) With armor
b) With thumb spikes
c) With horns

4. Which dinosaurs had horns and bony frills ?
a) *Velociraptors*
b) Ceratopsians
c) Utopians

What evidence is there?

A fossil found in Mongolia in 1971 showed a *Protoceratops* fighting like a rhinoceros, charging at a *Velociraptor* and smashing into it with its bony beak. The *Velociraptor*'s sharp claws had pierced the stomach and throat of the *Protoceratops*.

Which dinosaur used its head?

Pachycephalosaurus males had skulls with very thick tops. Rival males may have had head-butting contests to win a mate, like some wild sheep do today.

23

All Over the World

Maiasaura

Stegosaurus

This map shows where dinosaur fossils have been found. Experts have divided the dinosaur age into three main parts: the Triassic, Jurassic, and Cretaceous Periods. Different dinosaurs lived in each period, so some fossils are older than others.

Deinonychus

Diplodocus

Which dinosaurs have been found in North America?

Hundreds of dinosaur fossils, including *Diplodocus*, *Deinonychus*, and *Stegosaurus*, have been found in North America. The famous *Tyrannosaurus* and *Triceratops* have been found in North America, and nowhere else.

Cretaceous

Jurassic

Triassic

Which was the fiercest dinosaur in South America?

The biggest South American meat-eater found so far is *Piatnitzkysaurus*, which was about 20 feet long and 10 feet high. It chased and killed prey in the same way as its larger North American relative, *Allosaurus*.

Piatnitzkysaurus

Did some dinosaurs live all over the world?

Some dinosaurs, such as *Brachiosaurus*, have been found in North America, Africa, and Europe. Some dinosaurs have only been found on one continent.

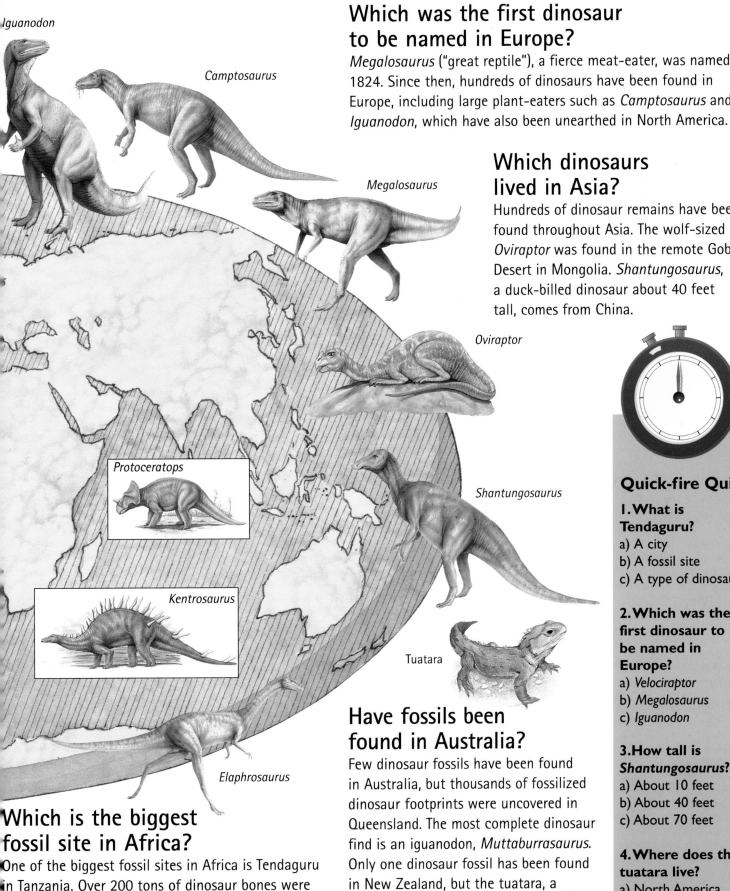

Iguanodon

Camptosaurus

Megalosaurus

Oviraptor

Protoceratops

Shantungosaurus

Kentrosaurus

Tuatara

Elaphrosaurus

Which was the first dinosaur to be named in Europe?

Megalosaurus ("great reptile"), a fierce meat-eater, was named in 1824. Since then, hundreds of dinosaurs have been found in Europe, including large plant-eaters such as *Camptosaurus* and *Iguanodon*, which have also been unearthed in North America.

Which dinosaurs lived in Asia?

Hundreds of dinosaur remains have been found throughout Asia. The wolf-sized *Oviraptor* was found in the remote Gobi Desert in Mongolia. *Shantungosaurus*, a duck-billed dinosaur about 40 feet tall, comes from China.

Have fossils been found in Australia?

Few dinosaur fossils have been found in Australia, but thousands of fossilized dinosaur footprints were uncovered in Queensland. The most complete dinosaur find is an iguanodon, *Muttaburrasaurus*. Only one dinosaur fossil has been found in New Zealand, but the tuatara, a reptile that lives there today, looks almost exactly the same as its ancestors that lived in the dinosaur age.

Which is the biggest fossil site in Africa?

One of the biggest fossil sites in Africa is Tendaguru in Tanzania. Over 200 tons of dinosaur bones were found there between 1909 and 1912. Many kinds of dinosaurs were dug up, including the stegosaur *Kentrosaurus* and the small, bird-like *Elaphrosaurus*.

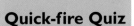

Quick-fire Quiz

1. What is Tendaguru?
a) A city
b) A fossil site
c) A type of dinosaur

2. Which was the first dinosaur to be named in Europe?
a) *Velociraptor*
b) *Megalosaurus*
c) *Iguanodon*

3. How tall is *Shantungosaurus*?
a) About 10 feet
b) About 40 feet
c) About 70 feet

4. Where does the tuatara live?
a) North America
b) Australia
c) New Zealand

Living in Herds

Clues such as footprints and mass dinosaur graves show that some dinosaurs lived in groups. Plant-eating dinosaurs probably herded together for safety, as antelope do today. Some meat-eaters may have hunted in packs.

Did herd members look after each other?

Fossilized footprints show that some dinosaur herds traveled with the young in the middle and the adults on the outside. If attacked, horned dinosaurs like *Triceratops* may have formed a circle around their young, with their horns pointing out toward the enemy, as musk oxen do today.

Which dinosaurs probably lived alone?

Large meat-eating dinosaurs such as *Albertosaurus* were excellent hunters and had few enemies. They could have lived and hunted alone, just as tigers do today. However, the bones of 40 young and adult *Allosaurus* were discovered in a group in the United States, so perhaps they hunted in packs like lions.

Why did dinosaurs live together?

Many plant-eaters, like these *Edmontosaurus* hadrosaurs, lived in herds for protection. Many eyes keeping watch for a predator is better than one pair. It is also more difficult for a predator to attack a large, moving herd. These hadrosaurs probably hooted and honked to signal to each other if there was danger, such as a carnosaur, nearby.

How do we know about dinosaur herds?

Vast tracks of fossilized dinosaur footprints all going the same way were discovered in North America. Experts believe they belonged to herds of dinosaurs. Huge numbers of dinosaurs have also been found buried together. One of these sites contained 10,000 duck-billed *Maiasaura*. This evidence shows that sauropods probably lived in groups.

Why did some herds die together?

In 1947, the fossilized remains of a large herd of *Coelophysis* were found at Ghost Ranch in New Mexico. The bones came from both young and old animals. Some experts think they probably all died together in a flash flood. Their bodies were carried along by the water and eventually dumped in a heap on a sandbank, where they fossilized.

Quick-fire Quiz

1. Where was a fossilized herd of *Coelophysis* found?
a) Ghost Ranch
b) Ghost Valley
c) Mexico Ranch

2. Which meat-eating dinosaur was found in a large group?
a) *Tyrannosaurus*
b) *Allosaurus*
c) *Diplodocus*

3. Why did *Edmontosaurus* herd together?
a) For company
b) For protection
c) To hunt

4. How many *Maiasaura* were found buried at one site?
a) 40
b) 1,000
c) 10,000

Did dinosaurs travel far?

Some dinosaurs, like these iguanodons, probably traveled huge distances in search of food. Today, animals such as caribou and wildebeests do the same.

Did herds migrate?

Probably. Dinosaurs have been found in the Arctic and Antarctic, where there would have been plenty of food in the summer, but little in the winter. Experts think that dinosaur herds migrated away from the poles in the winter, as modern-day caribou do.

Did dinosaur herds have lookouts?

No one knows for sure, but in large herds of animals, some adults keep watch for predators. Dinosaurs probably did the same.

Which dinosaurs hunted in packs?

Carnivores like wolves and hyenas hunt in packs. Many small meat-eating dinosaurs, such as *Elaphrosaurus*, probably hunted in packs too. This would have allowed them to hunt and kill larger prey than if they hunted alone.

Fast and Slow

A dinosaur's shape, size, and speed were determined by how it lived. Hunters had to be fast to catch their prey. They ran on strong back legs, using their tails for balance. Huge plant-eaters could only move slowly. They did not need to chase food, and their huge size kept them safe.

Iguanodon

Megalosaurus

How can we measure a dinosaur's speed?

Experts work out the speed at which a dinosaur moved from the space between its footprints and the length of its legs. The farther apart a dinosaur's tracks are, the faster it was moving. If the footprints are close together, it was probably walking slowly.

Which was the fastest dinosaur?

Ostrich-sized *Struthiomimus* was one of the fastest. It had no armor or horns to protect it and had to rely on speed to escape. It was as fast as a racehorse, reaching speeds of over 30 miles per hour.

What can footprints tell us?

Fossilized footprints can show how dinosaurs moved. For example, *Iguanodon* walked on all fours, but could run on its back legs. The huge, three-toed prints of *Megalosaurus* show that it was a meat-eater and always moved on its back legs.

How fast did dinosaurs move?

1 Just like animals today, dinosaurs moved at different speeds at different times. *Tyrannosaurus* walked at 10 miles per hour, but ran much faster when attacking.

2 *Hypsilophodon* was one of the speediest dinosaurs. This plant-eater could race along at up to 30 miles per hour to escape from enemies.

3 *Apatosaurus* weighed 40 tons— as much as seven elephants. It walked at 6 to 10 miles per hour. If it had tried to run, the impact would have broken its legs.

4 *Triceratops* weighed as much as five rhinoceroses. It could also charge like a rhinoceros at speeds of over 15 miles per hour. Few predators would risk attacking it.

Which was the slowest dinosaur?

The huge sauropods, like *Brachiosaurus*, were the slowest-moving dinosaurs. At over 50 tons, they were too heavy to run, so they plodded along at about 6 miles per hour. Unlike smaller dinosaurs, these huge creatures were probably too big to have reared up on their hind legs.

Warm or cold blood?

Mammals and birds are warm-blooded, which means they make their own body heat. Reptiles are cold-blooded and have to warm up in the sun. To get the energy to heat their bodies, warm-blooded animals need about ten times more food than a cold-blooded animal of the same size. Studying how much dinosaurs ate may show if any were warm-blooded.

In the Sea

While dinosaurs ruled the land, other giant reptiles took over the seas. Mosasaurs, plesiosaurs, and pliosaurs were fierce predators, snapping up fish and other sea creatures. Giant turtles and crocodiles also hunted in prehistoric oceans.

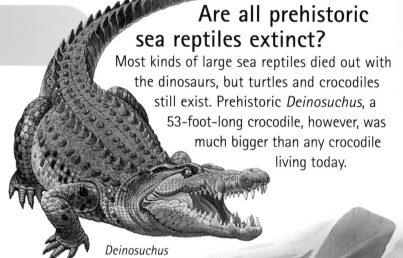

Are all prehistoric sea reptiles extinct?

Most kinds of large sea reptiles died out with the dinosaurs, but turtles and crocodiles still exist. Prehistoric *Deinosuchus*, a 53-foot-long crocodile, however, was much bigger than any crocodile living today.

Deinosuchus

Kronosaurus

Mosasaurus

What did sea reptiles eat?

Sea reptiles ate fish, shellfish, and even each other! A *placodont* picked up shellfish with its long front teeth. It crushed them with its back teeth, spat out the shells, and swallowed the rest.

Teleosaurus

Ammonite (swimming shellfish)

Placodont

Who was Mary Anning?

Mary Anning was born in 1799 in Dorset, England. She grew up to be a great fossil hunter and was so good that she earned her living by selling fossils. She found the first complete fossilized skeleton of a giant marine ichthyosaur when she was only 12 years old. Another of her amazing finds was the first complete skeleton of a plesiosaur.

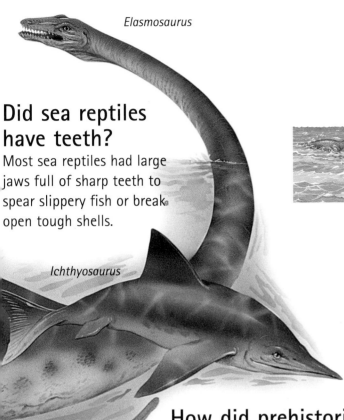
Elasmosaurus

Ichthyosaurus

Did sea reptiles have teeth?

Most sea reptiles had large jaws full of sharp teeth to spear slippery fish or break open tough shells.

Tanystropheus

Did any sea creatures come onto land?

Long-necked *Tanystropheus* hunted both on land and in the sea. It snapped up flying insects as well as slippery fish. Most sea reptiles had to come onto land to lay their eggs.

How did prehistoric sea reptiles swim?

Pliosaurs like *Kronosaurus* and plesiosaurs like *Elasmosaurus* had four strong paddles instead of feet. They moved them up and down to "fly" through the sea in the same way penguins do today. *Mosasaurus*, *Ichthyosaurus*, and crocodiles such as *Teleosaurus* swam by beating their tails from side to side. Sea reptiles could not breathe under water, so they swam to the surface to gulp in air.

Kronosaurus skeleton

How big were the sea reptiles?

One of the biggest sea reptiles was the pliosaur *Kronosaurus*. It was 55 feet long, with a huge head the size of a car. *Mosasaurus* was over 30 feet long, the largest lizard ever. Prehistoric turtles were also much bigger than their modern relatives. The largest, *Archelon*, was 13 feet long. Its huge front paddles powered it through the water at up to 10 miles per hour.

Archelon

Did sea reptiles lay eggs?

Most sea reptiles laid their eggs on land, like turtles today. But *Ichthyosaurus* gave birth to live young in the same way as sea mammals like this dolphin do today.

In the Air

When dinosaurs took over the land, other reptiles took to the air. The first reptiles to master flight were the pterosaurs. They ruled the skies for 166 million years, but died out at the end of the dinosaur age.

How big were pterosaurs?

Pterosaurs came in many sizes. *Quetzalcoatlus* was the largest. It had a human-sized body and a wingspan of over 40 feet—bigger than a hang glider! *Rhamphorhynchus* was the size of a crow, with a wingspan of 16 inches.

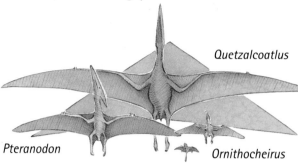

Quetzalcoatlus

Pteranodon

Ornithocheirus

Rhamphorhynchus

What did pterosaurs eat?

Pterosaurs' jaws and teeth help show what they ate. Most fed on fish, while some snapped up insects. *Pterodaustro* may have filtered tiny animals from the water with its sievelike bottom jaw. *Dzungaripterus*'s pincerlike beak could prise shellfish from rocks. *Dimorphodon*'s strong jaws were ideal for catching fish.

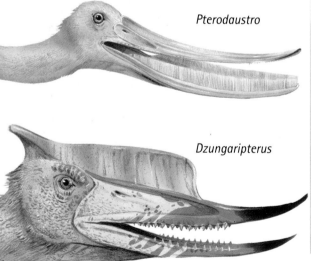

Pterodaustro

Dzungaripterus

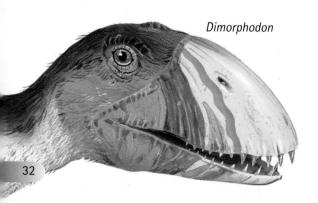

Dimorphodon

Pteranodon

Did pterosaurs build nests?

No one knows, but scientists think pterosaurs probably laid eggs. They may have laid them in nests and sat on them to keep them warm. Fossils show that baby pterosaurs were not well developed, so perhaps the adults fed them, as baby birds are fed today.

Furry and active?

Fossil evidence shows that some pterosaurs were covered with fur, which probably means they were warm-blooded, like birds. They also had big brains with large areas to control balance and sight.

When did reptiles first fly?

Reptiles first took to the air about 250 million years ago. Early flying reptiles, such as *Coelurosauravus*, were lizard-shaped with four legs. Their wings grew out from the sides of their bodies and were held rigid on long ribs. These reptiles used their wings to help them glide from tree to tree, but they could not flap them. One of the earliest gliding reptiles, *Longisquama*, had tall crests along its back. The crests may have opened out like wings to help it glide.

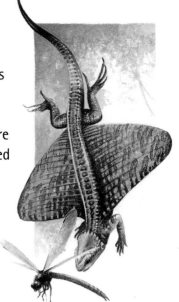
Coelurosauravus

Longisquama

Quetzalcoatlus

Quick-fire Quiz

1. Which was the largest pterosaur?
   a) *Pteranodon*
   b) *Quetzalcoatlus*
   c) *Pterodaustro*

2. What were pterosaurs' wings made of?
   a) Feathers
   b) Hair
   c) Skin

3. What did most pterosaurs eat?
   a) Fish
   b) Dinosaurs
   c) Insects

4. What were pterosaurs?
   a) Dinosaurs
   b) Reptiles
   c) Birds

Bat

Did pterosaurs have feathers?

Most pterosaurs were furry, not feathered, and their wings were made from sheets of leathery skin. In this way, they were more like bats than birds. The wings stretched from the pterosaur's body along its arm to the tips of its long fourth fingers. Their long wings were ideal for soaring on air currents.

Did pterosaurs have tails?

All pterosaurs had tails. Early kinds, such as *Dimorphodon*, had long tails to increase lift and help them steer. Later types, such as *Pteranodon*, were called pterodactyls. They had much bigger wings and tiny tails.

Death of the Dinosaurs

Dinosaurs died out about 65 million years ago. Studies show that they disappeared slowly in some places, but more suddenly in others. There are many theories to explain their extinction, but no one knows which is right.

Did a meteorite hit Earth?

One of the main theories is that a huge rock falling from outer space hit the earth. This meteorite threw up a cloud of dust, blocking out the sun's light and heat. The earth became much colder, and animals that could not cope with this died out. A huge crater that probably formed around this time has been found off the coast of Mexico. This evidence supports the idea that a meteorite caused the end of the dinosaurs.

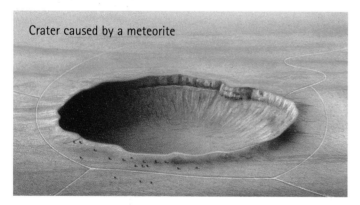
Crater caused by a meteorite

United States

Gulf of Mexico

✳ Impact site

Did mammals eat dinosaur eggs?

One explanation for the death of the dinosaurs is that the number of small mammals increased. The mammals ate so many dinosaur eggs that few babies hatched. There are many strange theories, and this is one of the more unlikely ones.

Did plant life change?

The extinction of dinosaurs and other animals may have been gradual. Towards the end of the dinosaur age, the tropical climate in North America became cooler and more seasonal, and tropical plants were replaced by woodland plants. The dinosaurs seem to have migrated south, so perhaps they could not adapt to these changes in climate and plant life.

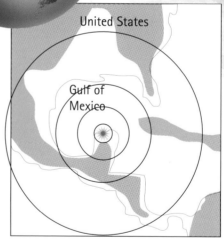

Did volcanoes make a difference?

Fossilized plant remains suggest that by 65 million years ago, the earth's climate had become cooler. Some scientists think this was caused by several huge volcanic eruptions that took place over a period of half a million years. Volcanoes send up gases and dust that can first heat the atmosphere, then cool it down, killing off life.

Were there other mass extinctions?

The end of the dinosaurs was not the first mass extinction. About 440 million years ago, almost half of the animal species died out, and another half died 370 million years ago. Over 95 percent of all living things died out about 345 million years ago, and 210 million years ago, at the end of the Permian Period, many land vertebrates died out. When these events happen, new species can take over the world.

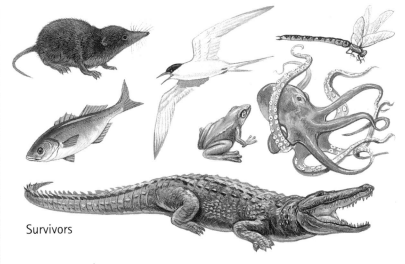

Survivors

Which animals died with the dinosaurs?

When the dinosaurs died out, so did many other reptiles, including mosasaurs, plesiosaurs, pliosaurs, and pterosaurs. Swimming shellfish like ammonites died too. Most other plants and animals, such as mammals, birds, frogs, fish, and other kinds of shellfish, survived. Not all reptiles died out either: turtles, crocodiles, snakes, and lizards still exist today.

Timescale

First life:
3.5 billion
years ago

The earth formed about 4.6 billion years ago, and life developed about 1 billion years later. The oldest known fossils, which are of shellfish, are 600 million years old. Dinosaurs arrived 230 million years ago, and the first true humans about 2 million years ago.

When did dinosaurs live?

The dinosaur age, the Mesozoic Era, lasted from 250 to 65 million years ago. Scientists split this time into three main periods. Dinosaurs first appeared in the **Triassic Period**, 230 million years ago. The continents were a single land mass called Pangaea ("All-earth"), and dinosaurs could roam all over the world. During the **Jurassic Period**, 145 million years ago, Europe and Africa began to move away from the Americas. In the **Cretaceous Period**, the land masses separated, and different dinosaurs developed on the different continents.

Triassic

Early Jurassic

Early Cretaceous

When did animals move onto land?

Life began in the sea. Animals first moved onto land about 380 million years ago. Amphibians like *Eryops* could breathe air, but like frogs and toads today, they had to return to water to lay their eggs and to keep their skin moist. *Eryops* was the size of a pig. Its thick skin protected it and helped support its body weight on land.

DEVONIAN

CARBONIFEROUS

Eryops

Which animals first lived on land?

Although amphibians could live on land, they were not true land animals, as they had to return to the water to breed. The tiny tadpoles that hatched had to stay in the water until they developed into adults. Reptiles were the first vertebrates (animals with backbones) that could live completely on land. They laid their leathery eggs on land, and the baby developed inside the egg, feeding on the yolk. The newly hatched baby was fully formed and active.

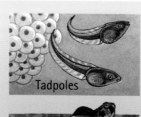
Tadpoles

Reptile hatching

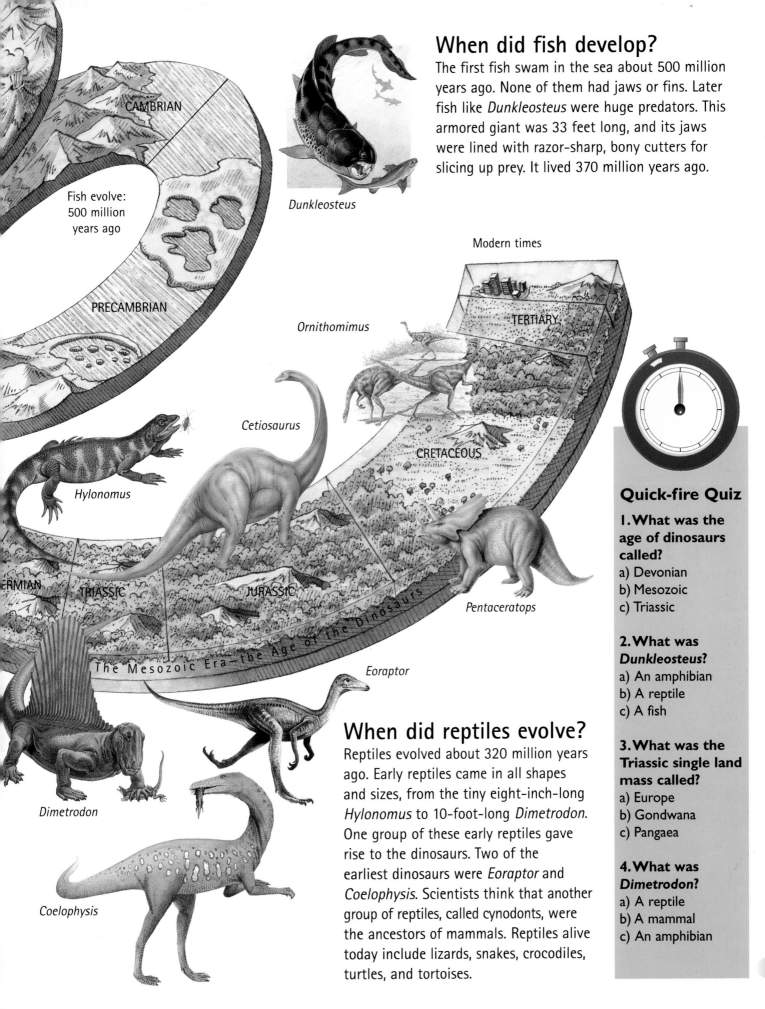

CAMBRIAN

Fish evolve:
500 million
years ago

PRECAMBRIAN

Dunkleosteus

When did fish develop?

The first fish swam in the sea about 500 million years ago. None of them had jaws or fins. Later fish like *Dunkleosteus* were huge predators. This armored giant was 33 feet long, and its jaws were lined with razor-sharp, bony cutters for slicing up prey. It lived 370 million years ago.

Modern times

Ornithomimus

TERTIARY

Cetiosaurus

CRETACEOUS

Hylonomus

Pentaceratops

ERMIAN TRIASSIC JURASSIC

The Mesozoic Era—the Age of the Dinosaurs

Eoraptor

Dimetrodon

Coelophysis

When did reptiles evolve?

Reptiles evolved about 320 million years ago. Early reptiles came in all shapes and sizes, from the tiny eight-inch-long *Hylonomus* to 10-foot-long *Dimetrodon*. One group of these early reptiles gave rise to the dinosaurs. Two of the earliest dinosaurs were *Eoraptor* and *Coelophysis*. Scientists think that another group of reptiles, called cynodonts, were the ancestors of mammals. Reptiles alive today include lizards, snakes, crocodiles, turtles, and tortoises.

Quick-fire Quiz

1. What was the age of dinosaurs called?
a) Devonian
b) Mesozoic
c) Triassic

2. What was *Dunkleosteus*?
a) An amphibian
b) A reptile
c) A fish

3. What was the Triassic single land mass called?
a) Europe
b) Gondwana
c) Pangaea

4. What was *Dimetrodon*?
a) A reptile
b) A mammal
c) An amphibian

After the Dinosaurs

After the dinosaurs died out, other animals developed to take their place. Warm-blooded mammals took over as the ruling animals. They dominated the land and even took to the air. A few even went to live in the place where life first developed—the ocean.

What are the dinosaurs' nearest surviving relatives?

Many scientists now agree that birds are the closest living relatives of the dinosaurs. The first bird fossil to be found was *Archaeopteryx*. It had a reptilelike skeleton similar to that of *Deinonychus* and feathered wings like a bird. *Archaeopteryx* had a long, bony tail, three clawed fingers on each hand, and teeth. Modern birds have lost their teeth and their clawed wing fingers. Their small tail stumps hold their tail feathers.

Deinonychus

What were early birds like?

Very few fossils of early birds have been found. Several almost complete skeletons of *Hesperornis*, a diving bird that lived at the end of the dinosaur age, were found in the United States. *Hesperornis*'s wings were so small that it was almost certainly flightless, but its large feet may have been webbed to help it swim. It looked much more like today's birds than *Archaeopteryx* did, but it still had teeth in its beak and a fairly long, bony tail.

Why were mammals so successful?

There are several reasons. Early mammals had bigger brains and were more intelligent than reptiles. They were hairy and warm-blooded, so they could live in colder places. Most of them cared for their young for a long time, so perhaps more young survived. Also, different mammal groups had different kinds of teeth, so they could feed on a huge range of food without competing with each other.

What were the first mammals like?

The first mammals evolved about 215 million years ago. One of the earliest known mammals is *Morganucodon*. This mouse-sized hunter was warm-blooded but probably laid eggs like the Australian platypus. *Zalambdalestes* lived at the same time as the last of the dinosaurs, and gave birth to live young.

Morganucodon

Zalambdalestes

Smilodon

Archaeopteryx

Pigeon

When did mammoths die out?

Woolly mammoths died out about 10,000 years ago. The giant North American mammoth was over 14 feet tall. These huge beasts were preyed on by *Smilodon*, a saber-toothed cat with fangs as long as your hand (6 inches). When the mammoths died out, so did *Smilodon*.

Mammoths

Late arrivals?

The first humans evolved about two million years ago, but modern humans, or *Homo sapiens* ("wise person"), only arose about 100,000 years ago. In the Stone Age, 20,000 years ago, people lived in caves and hunted with stone tools.

Quick-fire Quiz

1. Which of these have no teeth?
a) Modern birds
b) *Archaeopteryx*
c) *Hesperornis*

2. Which was the earliest known mammal?
a) Mammoth
b) *Smilodon*
c) *Morganucodon*

3. How long ago did modern humans evolve?
a) 20,000 years
b) 100,000 years
c) 5,000,000 years

4. Which animals dominated after the dinosaurs?
a) Mammoths
b) Amphibians
c) Mammals

Index

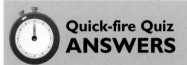

Quick-fire Quiz ANSWERS

Page 5 Digging up the Facts
1. b 2. c 3. c 4. b

Page 7 Color and Camouflage
1. b 2. a 3. b 4. a

Page 9 Dinosaur Giants
1. a 2. a 3. a 4. c

Page 11 Small Dinosaurs
1. c 2. c 3. a 4. b

Page 13 Dinosaur Babies
1. b 2. a 3. c 4. b

Page 15 Communication
1. a 2. a 3. c 4. b

Page 17 Plant-eaters
1. b 2. c 3. c 4. b

Page 19 Meat-eaters
1. c 2. c 3. b 4. a

Page 21 The Fiercest Dinosaur
1. b 2. c 3. b 4. b

Page 23 Attack and Defense
1. a 2. b 3. b 4. b

Page 25 All Over the World
1. b 2. b 3. b 4. c

Page 27 Living in Herds
1. a 2. b 3. b 4. b

Page 29 Fast and Slow
1. a 2. b 3. b 4. b

Page 31 In the Sea
1. c 2. a 3. c 4. b

Page 33 In the Air
1. b 2. c 3. a 4. b

Page 35 Death of the Dinosaurs
1. b 2. a 3. b 4. b

Page 37 Timescale
1. b 2. c 3. c 4. a

Page 39 After the Dinosaurs
1. a 2. c 3. b 4. c